Original title:
Acorn Anecdotes

Copyright © 2025 Creative Arts Management OÜ
All rights reserved.

Author: Helena Marchant
ISBN HARDBACK: 978-1-80567-198-5
ISBN PAPERBACK: 978-1-80567-497-9

Gentle Giants: Tales of the Timberland

In the shadow of trees, where the critters play,
Lived a squirrel named Frank, who danced every day.
He'd twirl on his tail, oh what a sight,
While the old oak would chuckle, 'You've got moves, alright!'

One day while he pranced, he stumbled and fell,
Right into a puddle—oh boy, what a smell!
The raccoons gathered round, all in a fuss,
Squeezing their cheeks, and made quite the fuss.

Frank shook off the mud, with a grin on his face,
"Who needs a shower? This is nature's embrace!"
The trees they all laughed, swaying side to side,
While the birds chirped a tune, their wings open wide.

Then came along Betty, the bear with a hat,
Who thought she could dance, but fell flat on her mat.
With a tumble and roll, she created a scene,
Leaving everyone giggling, oh what a queen!

So next time you visit the timberland's glee,
Remember the antics of friends wild and free.
Amongst all the giants, the laughter still lives,
In the stories they share, and the joy that it gives.

Shadows and Secrets of the Old Tree

Under the canopy wide and free,
Squirrels chatter, plotting a spree,
A hidden stash of nature's gold,
Secrets of the tree, they unfold.

Branches creak with tales so sly,
Of birdie plots and a butterfly,
A shadow dances, what a sight,
The old tree chuckles, day turns to night.

Echoes in Thickets and Glades

In the thicket, voices arise,
Whispers of mischief, oh what a prize!
The grass blades giggle, a lively crew,
While shadows chase a lost shoe.

Echoes bounce, with each rustle and move,
Chattering critters in playful groove,
A fox trips over a hidden root,
Nature's laughter, oh how cute!

Musings from the Rooted Realm

Beneath the bark, old stories bloom,
A wise old oak, filled with room,
For dreams of frogs on a lily pad,
And mysterious tales that make you glad.

Worms wiggle by, with secrets to keep,
While grasshoppers tap, in rhythms so deep,
Nature's gossip flies on a breeze,
Humor in the roots, it's sure to please.

Tales of Treetop Tumbles

Up high, the branches all sway,
Where birds complain of a bad hair day,
A clumsy raccoon stumbles near,
With each mishap, the laughter's clear.

Falling leaves, a golden parade,
Caught in the breeze, they twirl and fade,
The treetops giggle, just look at that!
Even the sun rises on a funny spat.

Nature's Well-Kept Stories

In the hush of trees so tall,
An acorn whispered its small call.
"I've seen squirrels play on high,
And chase their tails till they fly!"

The mushrooms giggled in a row,
"Watch out for rain! We learn, you know!"
They dance beside the wriggling snails,
And boast of their comical trails!

The Bounty Beneath the Earth

Underneath the leafy ground,
A treasure chest of oddities found.
Tubers talk of their fine bloom,
While roots tell jokes, shake off the gloom.

"Hey, sprout! You think you're all that?"
Said a radish to a curious brat.
"I'll grow taller than your tallest dreams,
And then I'll burst and fill the seams!"

Legends in Leaf and Limb

In the branches high, the stories weave,
A willow grins, all tricks up its sleeve.
"I saw a bird with shoes on tight,
Doing a jig from day to night!"

Foxes gossip in the cool, soft shade,
"There's mischief enough for the grand parade!"
They dance with shadows, play hide and seek,
While naughty elves spill tea, so to speak!

Small Wonders of the Forest

Tiny creatures of every kind,
Rabbits teasing, footloose and unconfined.
A chipmunk sings with a nutty flair,
"Who wore the best? You, or that hare?"

Each mushroom giggles, a mushroom band,
With funghi drums and shrooms so grand.
In this wood, laughter twinkles so bright,
With whispers of mischief in the soft moonlight.

Delicate Dramas in the Underbrush

In the thick of the green, a debate did arise,
A squirrel with a hat, and a crow in disguise.
They squabbled for hours, what a comical scene,
Over lost bits of cheese and a napkin of green.

The rabbit jumped in, with a wig on his head,
Claiming he owned all the crumbs that they fed.
But who knew that mushroom, so tall and discreet,
Had claimed all their cheer and their lunch in retreat!

Quirks of a Woodland Wanderer

There once was a chipmunk who fancied a shoe,
He wore it with pride, oh, what a view!
Yet each time he scurried, he stumbled and tripped,
A shoe full of nuts, oh how he whipped!

A deer joined his antics, with a scarf oh so bright,
They danced through the trees, what a delightful sight!
But tangled in branches, the shenanigans grew,
And laughter erupted; oh, what would they do?

The Journey into the Heart of Wood

A tale of a caterpillar craving delight,
He ventured so boldly into the night.
With dreams of a party, he sang with great flair,
But forgot he was munching on his own hair!

Through thickets and shadows, he met a wise frog,
"Your style's quite unique, but do lose that log."
With a hop and a skip, they pranced around,
Till a twig caught the caterpillar and down he found!

Stories etch'd on Leaves

Upon a leaf, a story was penned,
Of a robot of bark, who sought out a friend.
He tripped on a root, like a comic routine,
And fell in a puddle, all covered in green.

A wise old owl hooted, "Oh, what a trip!"
"Your circuits are funny; let's make you a script!"
With a wiggle and giggle, the forest drew close,
For laughter is magic, we treasure the most.

The Other Side of the Oak

An acorn tried to sing a tune,
But squirrels laughed beneath the moon.
They danced around, quite in a whirl,
    As that poor nut began to twirl.

A chipmunk asked, 'What's your plan?'
The acorn sighed, 'To be a man!'
But with no roots and all this fluff,
His dreams of growth were pretty tough.

With dreams of being tall and grand,
He learned the ground's a solid band.
He laughed it off, then rolled away,
And asked a tree, 'What's for lunch today?'

Narratives in Nature's Gentle Touch

There once was a nut, quite full of glee,
Claimed, 'I'll grow into a mighty tree!'
But winds of change blew in a rush,
And down he tumbled with a hush.

A butterfly swooped down for a chat,
'You're not alone, just look at that!'
They giggled about their lofty plight,
While grasshoppers joined in the light.

They spun a tale of dreams so bright,
Of dancing leaves and stars at night.
Our nut just chuckled, took a bow,
And wondered, 'What will come of me now?'

Lullabies of the Leafy Realm

In a woodland nook, a nut did sleep,
While cheeky critters made a leap.
With leaps and bounds, they shared their lore,
The acorn snoozed, dreaming of more.

A raccoon whispered, 'Let's play a game!'
The oak stood tall, but who took the blame?
A branch above, so wide and strong,
He worried, 'What if I don't belong?'

But laughter echoed in the trees,
As squirrels twirled in summer breeze.
'You'll be great!' the winds all cheered,
The future bright, no need to be feared.

The Forgotten Fables of the Woods

Deep in the woods, where shadows creep,
An acorn shared a secret deep.
'I've seen the world, I've rolled and rolled,
With tales of mischief yet untold!'

A fox replied, with a curious grin,
'What's so funny? Let the tales begin!'
And so they gathered, birds and beasts,
To hear of adventures, laughter, and feasts.

'The time I tried to jump a stream,'
Said the nut, 'I fell—oh what a dream!'
With every story, giggles grew,
The woods alive with joy anew.

A Journey of Roots and Wings

A tiny seed, dropped from heights,
Bounces down on sunny sights.
With dreams of trees, it starts to sprout,
But wonder where its friends have clout.

The wind's a friend, or so it claims,
It giggles loud, and plays some games.
From dirt it flies, to skies so blue,
But what's the point of being new?

Birds fly by with snappy jests,
While worms beneath just take their rests.
The sprout thinks fast, it needs a plan,
And hopes to grow as tall as man.

At last, it stands, a tree so fine,
With branches wide, and roots that shine.
It laughs at seeds that never took,
As squirrels scurry with their book.

Nature's Generations

There once was a nut, so round and cute,
Who dreamed of becoming a great big root.
He sat in the shade, with hopes so grand,
While critters laughed at his slight demand.

"Grow up!" the wise old oak did say,
"Stop dreaming dreams that fly away!
Just give it time, and you will see,
The world's much more than you and me."

So he sat and mused with a curious grin,
Imagined wings and a chance to win.
But like a tortoise, he moved real slow,
Still the funniest sprout to ever grow.

Then came a breeze that swayed him right,
He laughed so hard, he took to flight!
A tumble here, a twirl so grand,
His journey led to a wondrous land.

The Silent Watcher of Seasons

A wise old tree stood proud and tall,
With leaves like laughter, a leafy sprawl.
It listened to tales from sun and rain,
Of nuts that fell from their lofty chain.

"Hey there, tree! What do you spy?"
Said a squirrel, darting 'neath the sky.
"The seasons change, but you stay still,
What's it like to never thrill?"

The tree just chuckled, swayed its crown,
Watching the critters jump around.
"I've seen it all, from spring to frost,
But it's nature's winks that never cost."

So silent it stood, a keeper of lore,
As plants and animals danced and swore.
Yet deep down inside, it let out a sigh,
"Just let me grow, and I'll tell you why."

Secrets Beneath the Canopy

Under the leaves, a world so sly,
Where whispers and giggles often fly.
A band of bugs with secrets to keep,
In tunnels and roots, they laugh and peep.

"Did you hear about the nut so brave?"
Muttered a beetle, the gossip wave.
"It dreamed of wings, but only fell,
Now it's stuck in a funny shell."

A worm popped up, with a wink so sly,
"Let's tease the nut; oh my, oh my!"
They gathered round with laughter so slick,
As the nut complained, "You're being a trick!"

Yet shared in jest and wormy delight,
They spun a tale that lasted all night.
The secrets grew like roots in the ground,
Bound by humor, in friendship found.

Small Beginnings, Mighty Ends

In the ground where the critters play,
A tiny seed dreamt of a day.
It whispered, 'I might grow tall and wide,'
But first, it had to survive the ride.

A worm thought it'd make a great snack,
While squirrels were plotting a daring attack.
Yet with all the ruckus and din,
It sprouted a grin and said, "Let's begin!"

The sun waved down with a playful wink,
The rain joined in, giving a drink.
Roots dug deep, it began to sway,
"Just wait, my friend—I'll steal the day!"

With each passing season, it grew more bold,
A tale of a hero, waiting to unfold.
From a simple seed to a towering trend,
It laughed, "See? Small starts can lead to big ends!"

Budding Stories Beneath the Bark

Beneath the bark, where secrets spill,
Little tales hide, waiting until.
A chipmunk once thought he'd take a peek,
But shivers of laughter made him squeak.

The mushrooms chuckled, the grass had a ball,
As branches danced low, giving it all.
"Did you hear the one about the tree?
It tried to blow away like a leaf, you see!"

With whispers of winds and tales of trees,
The woodland critters giggled with ease.
"Remember the time when a branch went kaput?
It landed on a toad, and oh, what a hoot!"

So next time you wander through forest paths,
Keep an ear open for nature's laughs.
In stories beneath the bark, you'll find,
The funny side of life, intertwined.

The Chronicles of a Tiny Seed

A tiny seed, in the cool, damp dirt,
Dreamed of days that weren't besmirched.
"Just wait 'til I grow, I'll be a tree!"
But first, it had to dodge a bee!

With chuckles of grass and giggles of dew,
It wriggled and wobbled, oh, what a view!
"Careful!" cried a snail with a snicker.
"That bird up there? It's quite the flicker!"

As summer rolled in, with warmth in the air,
It poked through the soil, rejoicing, aware.
"What's this? A flower? I'm not alone!"
"Oh no!" said the flower, "I'm just a loan!"

Yet through trials and laughs, it pushed ahead,
Storms couldn't dampen the jokes that it spread.
From a silly seed to a tree with a bend,
The chronicles of growth, Fun never ends!

Woodland Memoirs

In the woods where the hiccups of creatures nest,
A memoir of laughter unfolds as the best.
There's Benny the beetle, who thinks he can fly,
But mostly just twirls, oh me, oh my!

The owls tell tales that makes squirrels cheer,
About a raccoon who swiped a cold beer.
"Do you remember," they croon, so alive,
"When he tried to hiccup and got a high five?"

The dewdrops giggle as sunlight spills,
Over stories and secrets of woodland thrills.
A dance party starts with a butterfly glide,
"Join in!" call the daisies, "We'll never hide!"

So when you stroll down those leafy lanes,
Remember the joy that silly fun gains.
In woodland memoirs, humor unbends,
Every moment's a treasure—this joy never ends!

Gentle Whispers of the Woods

In the shade, the critters grin,
Beneath a tree, where tales begin.
A squirrel shimmies, steals a snack,
While owls argue, 'Who's got the knack?'

The breeze brings giggles, secrets shared,
A worm wears glasses, feeling prepared.
Rabbits dance in their little suits,
As mushrooms gossip in tiny boots.

Frogs leap high, with cotton tails,
While raccoons plot their nighttime sales.
The trees shake heads, with leaves that sway,
"And here they come, what a silly day!"

So in the woods, where laughter dwells,
Each creature spins their funny spells.
The shadows chuckle, light beams play,
In this wild world, let joy lead the way.

Little Giants of the Forest

Tiny seeds sprout, oh what a sight,
They reach for the sky, in pure delight.
With dreams of grandeur, they stretch so wide,
While chipmunks cheer, and squirrels slide.

"Just watch us grow!" the seedlings shout,
As ants parade, all marching out.
A beetle sports a tiny crown,
Declaring, "I am king, don't frown!"

Mice host parties near a stout oak,
While feisty rabbits pull their cloak.
Every creature plays a part,
In this grand race, who's got the heart?

So here's to those small but bold,
With stories of laughter, yet untold.
In every corner, joy ignites,
With little giants reaching new heights.

The Life Cycle of a Tiny Marvel

From hushed beginnings in the earth,
A tiny seed finds its new birth.
With sunlight's kiss, and rain's embrace,
It stretches forth, claiming its space.

A sprout emerges, wears a cap,
And soon enough, takes a nap.
Curly and twisty, it grows so tall,
While bunnies cheer, "You'll never fall!"

Time ticks by, with laughter and glee,
As leaves unfurl, oh can't you see?
The sky's its friend, the wind's a tease,
"Hold on tight," it shouts with ease.

So watch it dance, this tiny sprout,
A hero in green, without a doubt.
Through funny fables, it finds its way,
In nature's realm, all here to play.

Nature's Keepers: A Silent Ode

In hushed tones, the woods speak clear,
Of tiny tales, we hold so dear.
The ants in lines, a grand parade,
While leaves chuckle, quite unafraid.

Old wineskin trees, full of stories,
Whispering softly of nature's glories.
The mushrooms wink, with laughter muted,
To passing bugs, who feel quite rooted.

Each pebble grins, beneath the moss,
Hiding secrets, without a gloss.
The wind carries giggles, through the air,
As sunlight filters, without a care.

So here's to those keepers of lore,
Whispering tales, forevermore.
In every rustle and gentle sigh,
Nature's humor will never die.

When Wind Whispers

When wind whispers soft and clear,
Little nuts hide, filled with fear.
They roll and bounce with every gust,
Oh, where will they land? They must adjust.

The squirrel laughs from his high perch,
As nuts get tossed, they start to lurch.
One lands in a patch of moss,
The others claim it's all a toss!

With every twist, they learn to sway,
Chasing laughter along the way.
Just a game of windy fun,
Each nut giggles, not on the run.

So when you hear the breezy calls,
Remember nuts in glory stalls.
With every woosh, they dance with glee,
Just don't forget to watch the tree!

The Life of a Leaf in Fall

A leaf once bright, took quite a turn,
Fell from the branch, with much to learn.
Spinning down in a swirling dance,
It shouted out, 'I'll take my chance!'

'This ground is soft, a cozy bed!'
Said the leaf, as the squirrels fled.
A picnic spread, just for me,
Amidst the crunching, so carefree.

Then came the rain, oh what a splash!
Turns out, puddles weren't so brash.
'Surf's up!' the leaf yelled with delight,
While critters warned, 'Ah, hold on tight!'

With every gust, it laughed and twirled,
'This leaf life, my friends, is quite a world!'
So next fall season, join the spree,
And let the leaf set your heart free!

The Nut that Dreamed of Greatness

A nut sat dreaming on the ground,
Of grand adventures all around.
'One day, I'll be a mighty tree,
Just wait and see, you'll envy me!'

It plotted and planned with silly flair,
Wishing for roots, a trunk, and hair.
But when it tried to dig a hole,
It stumbled hard, oh what a toll!

A wise old owl saw the mess,
Said, 'Dear nut, it's okay to rest.'
'You'll grow one day, just give it time,
And while you wait, enjoy this rhyme.'

So, under the stars, the nut would grin,
'Who needs to rush, when dreams begin?'
With laughter shared among the critters,
The nut forgot all about the jitters!

Fables from the Forest Floor

Down on the floor where critters play,
Fables burst forth in a funny way.
A toadstool's tale, a tale so bold,
Of escapades both bright and old.

A snail with dreams of speed so grand,
Challenged the rabbit for a race so planned.
With giggles and grins, they took their mark,
But the snail, alas, was late, oh hark!

A wise old turtle watched and sighed,
'This is the forest, where fun won't hide.'
With laughter ringing through the trees,
Each creature joins in, feeling the breeze.

So gather 'round, my friends, take heed,
In the forest floor, there's always a need.
To share a tale, a giggle, a cheer,
Where every fable brings joy near!

Underneath the Ancient Oaks

Underneath the ancient oaks,
The squirrels tell silly jokes,
They dance and prance, with little fear,
While wise old owls just scratch an ear.

The sunbeams play hide and seek,
A chipmunk whispers, 'I'm so sleek!'
But tripping roots cause lots of fuss,
As fluffy tails go flying thus.

Acorns drop like tiny bombs,
Sprouting dreams of future farms.
Each nut dreams of a mighty tree,
While giggles echo, wild and free.

And if you listen close enough,
You'll hear the trees say, 'Life's tough!'
Yet laughter wins the forest fight,
In this grand tale of pure delight.

Dreams of an Oak Leaf

A leaf dreamed it could fly so high,
With feathered friends up in the sky.
It flapped and flopped, but fell with grace,
Landing with laughter, on a mushroom's face.

Nearby a snail shared a joke so grand,
'Why walk slow, when you can glide on sand?'
The leaf just giggled, not one bit shy,
'I'll get my wings, just you wait and try!'

Each dawn it winked at the rising sun,
Hoping for winds, to join the fun.
Yet every time, its dreams would fade,
While ants danced circles, unafraid.

So now it rests beneath the boughs,
Content to watch all creatures' wow.
With happy heart, it whispers low,
'Life's a party, give it a go!'

The Journey of a Little Seed

A little seed had dreams so wide,
'I'll travel far, I'll take a ride!'
It rolled and tumbled down the hill,
Until a gust gave it a thrill.

It bounced through flowers, oh so bright,
Giggling loudly at the sight.
'Look at me, I'm on a spree!'
Said the little seed with glee.

A butterfly danced to lead the way,
While ladybugs joined in the play.
Before it knew, it took a leap,
Landed in soil, so warm and deep.

Now planted firm, it smiles with glee,
'One day I'll be a mighty tree!'
With roots that laugh and branches that sway,
In this grand woodland, I'll surely stay.

Secrets of the Forest Floor

Beneath the leaves and twigs galore,
Lie secrets wrapped in nature's lore.
A family of mushrooms start to talk,
Sharing stories of the woodland walk.

'Why did the tree cross the stream?'
It wanted to fulfill its dream!'
The berries burst out in glee,
'The more, the merrier, can't you see?'

The beetles roll the tiny gnomes,
Playing hide and seek in their homes.
Every rustle brings a laugh,
For joy is found in nature's path.

With laughter echoing through the trees,
Even the shadows join the breeze.
In every nook, a cheer so bright,
On this enchanted forest night.

A Symphony of Seedlings

In the shade, a tiny sprout,
Sings a tune with leaves about.
Wiggling roots, a joyful dance,
Tickling soil, given a chance.

Sprinkled rain like giggly drops,
Each bud pops, and never stops.
Buds on branches, full of glee,
Nature's concert, come and see!

Squirrels jam with acorns bold,
Playing beats, their stories told.
Nature's band, a sight to hear,
Rooted friends, bring laughs and cheer!

With each breeze, they sway and prance,
Join the show, don't miss your chance.
A seedling's life is never bland,
From small things, big laughs are planned.

Nature's Little Memoirs

Once was a seed, a hopeful dream,
Pitched to the sky, it made a beam.
Told the stories of summer's pride,
Of sunshine, growth, and a wild ride.

With winds that tickled every bud,
It penned down tales of mud and flood.
A caterpillar's slip and slide,
Written in leaves, they giggle and glide.

Among the branches, critters convene,
Sharing punchlines, if you know what I mean.
Eager squirrels with their cheeky schemes,
Live out loud, in nature's sweet dreams.

Each story told as the sun dips low,
A laughter-filled saga, in evening's glow.
The whispers of plants keep the antics alive,
Nature's memoirs make us thrive.

The Grit of Growing Up

A little sprout pushed through the ground,
Faced the world, what joy it found!
With bold ambition and silly flair,
Popping up and shedding care.

Chased by winds, a hapless feat,
Dancing round on tiny feet.
Bundles of leaves and a slightly bent spine,
Growing up's a wobbly line!

Each bug that passes shares a tale,
Some get stuck, others sail.
Grumpy bugs and chirpy tunes,
Nature's humor fills the afternoons.

The sun can smile or throw a frown,
Yet still, the rose wears a crown.
With laughter ringing, the roots take hold,
Life's adventures never get old!

Timeless Tales from the Trunk

In the heart of woodland, stories weave,
Old trunks chuckle, believe!
Each knot and swirl, a laugh in time,
Recalling squirrels' grandest climbs.

When storms approached, they hid in fright,
But soon found joy in stormy night.
The echoes of thunder caused such a cheer,
Branches swayed, but they had no fear!

With every ring, tales unfold,
Of past mischief, brave and bold.
Raccoons giggle with twinkling eyes,
As they raid the pantry of surprise.

So gather 'round the towering trees,
Listen close to the woodland breeze.
For every laugh, a story awaits,
Timeless humor, where nature relates.

The Secret Life of Seeds

In the dark of the earth, they giggle,
Dreaming of growing up big and spry.
Watching the squirrels shuffle and wiggle,
While plotting their ways to the sky.

With whispers of winds so crisp and bright,
They twirl around in a leafy dance.
Chasing away the day and night,
Each seed holds its hidden romance.

From tiny specks they sprout with glee,
Swinging on branches, carefree and bold.
Tales of adventures, just wait and see,
As they stretch and reach, they break the mold.

So next time you wander through trees,
Remember the laughter deep in the ground.
Those little seeds, just laughing with ease,
Are having the best time all around.

Buried Dreams of the Forest

Deep underground, where the shadows play,
Dreams of mighty oaks start to bloom.
They chuckle at squirrels who scamper away,
Thinking they're safe in their leafy room.

Each little seed has a tale to tell,
Of wacky winds and rain that's a blast.
They giggle at saplings who trip and fell,
Sharing the fun of their leafy past.

As the sun spills warmth in a joyful way,
Roots twist and tangle in a playful spree.
They tease the mushrooms, soft and gray,
In this wild, whimsical jubilee.

So if you listen close, you might find,
The secrets in soil, where stories reside.
Nature's giggles echo, intertwined,
In a world where dreams will never hide.

Little Stories from the Woodland

Under the canopy, funny tales emerge,
Of brave little seeds with lofty dreams.
They sandcastle-build in a muddy surge,
And race with the beetles in wobbly gleams.

Each whispering leaf tells a joke or two,
While squirrels prepare for a seed-collecting spree.
The laughter of branches blends with the dew,
In a bustling forest, wild and free.

As branches yawn and stretch wide in the sun,
The forest creates a whimsical show.
Nutty contests of who has the most fun,
While shadows below steal the bright glow.

So come and join in, don't miss the play,
For every seed has a story to spin.
The woodland's a stage where the laughter will sway,
And the fun never ends; it's where we begin.

Rustic Chronicles of the Nut

Gather 'round, let's spin a yarn,
About nuts that think they're the bees' knees.
With capes made of shells, they strut on the lawn,
And brag about traveling with the breeze.

In their secretive world, no tale is too grand,
Adventures on branches and leaps from high logs.
Challenging squirrels with a delicate hand,
While mocking the slugs and the lazy old frogs.

When winds start to whistle and dance in the night,
These rascally nuts play hide and seek.
With giggles and grins, they relish the fright,
As the moon lights their antics, cheeky and sleek.

So next time you snack on a roasted delight,
Think of the tales that critters will share.
For each nut holds a secret, like stars in the night,
In rustic chronicles that dance through the air.

Rooted in Mystery: A Testament

Beneath the ground, secrets lie,
Tiny tales that make us sigh.
What dreams do small seeds dare to share?
Whispers of squirrels, flying through air.

In the shade, laughter does play,
As critters claim the sunlit bay.
Growing tall, with stories to tell,
Who knew roots could weave such a spell?

Nature's jesters, so full of glee,
Juggling acorns, wild and free.
Two squirrels race, and oh, they trip,
Landing hard in a leafy slip!

Old shadows dance when winds do blow,
The riddle of growth, we still don't know.
Yet joy sprouts from the strangest nook,
Life's playful chapter, a comic book.

The Bark's Soft Stories

Upon the bark, tales are drawn,
Of mischief that greets each dawn.
Woodpeckers knock, a rhythmic tap,
While sleepy owls take a gentle nap.

Rabbits hop, with laughter bright,
As they peek from bushes, sheer delight.
Every knot and hole a stage,
For nature's antics to engage.

In the dusk, the shadows play,
Squirrels chase their blues away.
With each giggle from the tree,
Life's funny moments come to be.

As branches sway, the stories spin,
Of cheeky foxes with a grin.
So listen close when winds do call,
For nature's humor enchants us all.

Mischief in the Trunk

A little bug went on a spree,
Declared itself the king of glee.
It danced around a wooden rail,
While leaf-blowers unleashed their gale.

The trunk, it creaked with laughter loud,
At antics of the roaming crowd.
Chipmunks darted, tails held high,
Whilst bees buzzed baffled, oh my, oh my!

With sticky sap like silly glue,
The bugs all mocked the birds in blue.
"Your music's sweet, but guess who's king?"
A butterfly laughed, "Oh, what a fling!"

Just when the sun began to rest,
The mischief grew, they liked it best.
In twilight's glow, with twinkling eyes,
Nature's pranks spark joyful surprise.

The Wisdom of the Old Oak

The old oak sits, a jovial sage,
With stories spun, page by page.
Its branches sway with ancient grace,
Guarding tales of nature's space.

"Gather 'round!" it seems to say,
As critters lounge at end of day.
"Let me share my timeless lore,
Of funny things that came before!"

Once a worm, who thought it grand,
Took a dance on a sunny strand.
But slipped and fell, oh what a sight!
Laughter rang from morning to night.

Now squirrels pause when the wind talks,
As if it knows all of life's flocks.
So if you're near, lend an ear close,
For wisdom lies in nature's dose.

Tributes to Tiny Generations

In the tiny caps, they wear with pride,
 Little soldiers, in the forest, hide.
With faces small, and mighty dreams,
 They giggle loud, or so it seems.

Each one a plan, a grand design,
As they march forth, in a straight line.
They whisper tales of legendary fate,
A little squirrel just stole their plate.

In every nook, their laughter rings,
Pretending to be the kings of things.
While elders scoff at what they see,
 A tiny world, full of glee.

So here's a toast to the pint-sized crew,
Who plot and scheme on morning dew.
 With courage bold, and little cheer,
 The tiny ones bring us joy each year.

The Unsung Heroes of Shade

Beneath the trees, they take their stand,
The smallest nuts, oh, isn't it grand?
They labor hard to grow and sprout,
While big old oaks just stretch about.

They dodge the rain, and scurry away,
When wind whips up, it's not their day.
With roots entwined in laughter's hold,
In games of hide-and-seek, they're bold.

Though underfoot, they bind the ground,
In every stumble, their tales abound.
To shade our heads, they quietly fight,
While we enjoy the sunlight bright.

So tip your hat to the little ones,
The hidden tribe of fake old puns.
In the dance of leaves, let's all partake,
And thank the nuts for shade, not flake.

From Grounded Dreams to Great Heights

From dusty earth, they spy the sky,
With little hopes, they leap and fly.
In every pit, a dream is sewn,
While pranks unfold, their tales are grown.

Each tiny hat, a crown they bear,
They stretch their limbs, with dreams to share.
Competing to be the tallest sprout,
With goofy poses, there's no doubt.

They swing and sway, with glee they laugh,
Creating chaos in their path.
Who knew a nut could bring such fun,
While dancing 'neath the warming sun?

So here's to dreams that grow so wild,
In every seed, there's still a child.
With roots so deep, and spirits high,
They'll reach the stars, there's no deny.

Strands of Time in the Underbrush

In shady spots where secrets lie,
Little tales spin, oh my, oh my!
Nuts gather round, to spin a yarn,
Of daring deeds, by noon and dawn.

Twirling tales of squirrels bold,
In every shade, adventure's told.
From bumpy rides on beetle backs,
To hiding spots from cheeky jacks.

With laughter shared among the leaves,
A chorus rises, no one grieves.
For time is woven, here and now,
In every nut, there's room to plow.

So raise a cheer for roots below,
Where sticky dreams and giggles flow.
In every nut, love's serenade,
In the underbrush, life's grand parade.

Dusty Paths and Nutty Wisdom

Down the old path, a nutty point,
A squirrel stumbles, falls on a joint.
He shakes it off, then looks around,
In this silly world, laughter is found.

With a wiggle and jiggle, he takes a chance,
The trees all giggle, enjoying the dance.
A mischievous breeze, it starts to tease,
Whirling leaves, bringing playful unease.

Under the shade, wisdom is shared,
A critter's tale, none are spared.
From tiny seeds to tales so grand,
All living beings lend a hand.

So tread lightly on dusty trails,
For laughter's lurking, where humor prevails.
Each nut holds a story, quirky and bright,
In nature's embrace, we find pure delight.

Telltales from the Treetops

From the topmost branch, the gossip flies,
Birds sharing secrets with mischievous sighs.
A raccoon listens, feigning a yawn,
While the wise old owl hoots at dawn.

"Did you hear the joke?" chirps a lively thrush,
"Of the squirrel who thought he'd learned how to hush!"
With a flap and a flutter, the news spreads wide,
As laughter cascades down the leafy slide.

Treetops are bustling, chatter galore,
Each rustle and whisper opens a door.
With a tongue-in-cheek twist, they revel in mirth,
A canopy of laughter, an orchard of worth.

So next time you wander, glance up and see,
The bundled-up jokes that reside in the tree.
For every rustling leaf holds a giggle or two,
A chorus of chuckles, awaiting for you.

The Burgeoning Legacy of Trees

In the heart of the grove, where whispers dwell,
Old trunks tell stories, can't you tell?
With rings like laugh lines, they share their days,
Memories tangled in their leafy ways.

A squirrel claimed fame for his nutty feat,
But tripped on a branch with two left feet.
Laughter erupted from roots deep and wide,
As the trees joined in, filling hearts with pride.

Under a grand oak, kids play hide and seek,
Branches overhead, nature's grand peek.
Each laugh echoes through the boughs up high,
A legacy thriving, reaching the sky.

So remember, dear friend, as seasons turn,
The tales of the trees, for wisdom we yearn.
With laughter and joy, they grow ever tall,
Sharing their quirks, embracing us all.

Surreptitious Secrets of Ancient Oaks

In the shadowy depths where secrets brew,
The ancient oaks whisper, just for a few.
With twinkling bark and a knowing grin,
They tell the best tales of where they've been.

"Did you see that bird?" one tree softly speaks,
"Thought he could dance, but he tripped on his beak!"
Laughter echoes among the leaves' sway,
As secrets of life keep boredom at bay.

Mischief unfolds in the dappled light,
A squirrel tries juggling, oh what a sight!
The acorns all giggle, rolling with glee,
In the company of friends, how happy they be.

So venture with caution, in their embrace,
For every fable brings a smile to your face.
In the heart of the woods, where laughter won't cease,
The ancient oaks guard joy, like a sweet peace.

Musical Notes from the Canopy

Up in the branches, they strum and they hum,
Squirrels tap dance, while the woodpecker drums.
Leaves flutter softly, join in on the fun,
A concert of critters, under the sun.

A barking dog joins, he thinks he's a star,
He howls out a tune, from near and far.
The rabbits jump in, with a beat of their feet,
Creating a rhythm, that's truly a treat.

A squirrel lost focus, fell right on the ground,
Still bops to the music, as all laugh around.
Nature's own symphony, no tickets required,
Just come with a smile, and your joy will be inspired.

So next time you wander, look up and you'll see,
The critters, the laughter, a wild jamboree.
With music and magic, they sway in the trees,
Nature's own gig, bringing everyone ease.

Chronicles of Nature's Mirth

Once in a forest, a frog had a dream,
To croak out a tune, and create a big scheme.
He called up the birds, for a wonderful jam,
But the first note he hit? Turned out to be spam.

A turtle named Timmy, slow but quite wise,
Laughed at the frog, with bright twinkling eyes.
"We can't make a band, if the lead singer croaks!"
Then all of the critters burst out into jokes.

A beaver with talent, began to build props,
A stage made of branches, where laughter never stops.
The rabbit was baking, sweet treats on display,
But forgot the sugar, oh what a cliché!

At dusk, as they gathered, the show came alive,
With frogs, birds, and turtles, their spirits would thrive.
A night filled with laughter, it surely was worth,
The funniest tales of this whimsical earth.

The Nut's Remarkable Journey

There once was a nut, quite round and so bold,
Decided to travel, a story to unfold.
He rolled down the hillside, with giggles galore,
Until he found trouble, and bumped into a door.

The doorknob chuckled, said, "What brings you here?"
The nut, feeling cheesy, replied without fear.
"I'm on a grand quest, making friends as I roll,
To find laughter's cathedral, that's my ultimate goal!"

He sailed past a stream, where fish flashed a grin,
"Why swim, little nut? Just take it all in!"
The nut laughed aloud, splashing waves for a play,
Living life on the edge, come what may.

Then, out of the blue, he met a wise tree,
"You've journeyed much farther than most nuts, you see.
Just share your fun tales, and laughter you'll find,
True joy in the journey, you leave behind!"

Fleeting Moments Among the Pines

In the shade of the pines, where shadows dance bright,
An old chipmunk basked in the soft morning light.
With a wink of his eye, he shared a tall tale,
Of a nut on a journey, that followed a snail.

The snail, with a grin, said, "I'm fast, can't you see?"
As he inched past the chipmunk, oh what a spree!
They laughed and they chortled, their joy wasn't shy,
Underneath the green canopy, time flew right by.

A crow cawed a joke about shoes without lace,
The laughter erupted, it was quite the embrace.
Then a squirrel chimed in, with a wiggle and twist,
"Let's dance in the branches, we surely must whisk!"

As dusk started creeping, and shadows grew long,
They sang out their songs, as a whimsical throng.
Among laughter and joy, the day settled fine,
A moment well spent, this world of the pine.

Journeys of a Falling Leaf

A leaf once dreamed of being high,
In breezy dances, it learned to fly.
With spins and twirls, it took a dive,
And giggled, "Finally, I'm alive!"

It landed on a dog's wet nose,
"Excuse me, sir, but here's my prose!"
The pup just sneezed, barked out loud,
The leaf flew up, feeling quite proud.

It rode the wind above the stream,
Where fish looked up and joined the dream.
"Hey, water sprites, let's have some fun!"
And twirling twigs joined in, one by one.

With each small gust, it sailed away,
Eager to embrace the day.
From cloud to tree, its journey grand,
A tip of nature's hat, so unplanned!

The Oak's Silent Witness

The old oak tree stood tall and wise,
With branches wide, it spied the skies.
A squirrel danced upon its trunk,
While cracking jokes, it laughed and shrunk.

"Hey, acorn, why so round and meek?"
"I'm saving up for winter's peak!"
The acorn replied with a sassy glee,
"As if you'd understand what it means to be free!"

A bird flew by, a feathered grand,
"Got a seed that's simply unplanned!
What if I take your buddy away?"
The oak just chuckled, "Good luck today!"

The branches rustled with hidden mirth,
Squirrels scolded, "We'll still have worth!"
As acorns watched from their lofty perch,
The oak laid back, just enjoying the church.

Beneath the Bark: A Memoir

Beneath the bark, there's much to find,
An old snail's tale, all intertwined.
"I slid through rain, I crawled through dust,
Got licked by frogs—it's quite a must!"

The beetles laughed, chattered away,
"Your slow-paced life is quirky ballet!"
With flashes of wings above its head,
The snail just shrugged, "I'd rather tread."

A wise old worm popped in for tea,
"Let's toast our lives, what's life to be?"
He spilled the drink on a small ant's shoe,
"Oops, pardon me! Oh, what a view!"

And there in laughter, nature's jest,
Each little bug felt truly blessed.
With stories shared in friendship's embrace,
Life beneath the bark was a silly race.

Nature's Smallest Legends

In the heart of woods, tales come alive,
With tiny heroes who strive and thrive.
A gopher once tried to dig a hole,
And found a stash from a lost squirrel's soul.

"I swear I didn't mean to rob,"
He squeaked in protest, a guilty mob.
But the squirrel grinned, "You found my stash!
Just let me in for a giant bash!"

A ladybug boasted tales so tight,
"I've flown through storms, I've seen the light!"
But when a gust sent her spiraling down,
She laughed, "Next time I'll wear a crown!"

From mushrooms to moss, stories unfold,
In shades of green, legends retold.
So join their whimsy and take a chance,
For nature's smallest legends love to dance!

From Ground to Greatness

Once a little seed so small,
Dreamed of growing proud and tall.
But a squirrel dashed right by,
Scooped him up, oh my, oh my!

In a pocket snug and tight,
He pondered all his dreams at night.
'Will I be a tree or just a snack?'
He sighed and hoped to make it back.

But adventure called him forth,
And showed him the forest's worth.
From nutty tales to woodland fun,
He learned that every journey's won!

Finally planted, he stood so proud,
Rooted deep in the merry crowd.
No longer just a tiny shell,
He found his greatness, oh so well!

Woodland Wonders Unfold

In a glade where tall trees sway,
Lived a nut who wished to play.
'What if I could roll away,
And join the critters, bright and gay?'

He tumbled down a sunny hill,
Spun and twirled with girlish thrill.
A rabbit laughed and joined the race,
Chasing dreams, like they'd won first place!

From branch to root, they zipped around,
Chasing shadows on the ground.
Until they found a tiny brook,
Where giggles danced like storybooks.

As evening neared and stars appeared,
Our nutty friend cheered, unfeared.
For laughter echoed through the night,
In woodland wonders, pure delight!

The Oak's Gentle Wisdom

An old oak spoke with rustling leaves,
'Listen close, my tiny thieves.
Life's a journey, full of cheer,
But don't get too cozy, my dear!'

Young nuts gathered, hopeful and bold,
'Tell us tales of dreams untold!'
Said the oak with a gentle grin,
'Sometimes you lose, that's how you win.'

A fallen acorn, feeling blue,
Asked the oak, 'What should I do?'
'Just lay low, embrace the ground,
In time, your strength will come around.'

The wisdom sprouted, hearts took flight,
A nut's journey felt just right.
With roots so deep, and spirits high,
They laughed and reached for the sky!

Nutty Tales of the Forest

There once was a nut named Chuck,
With dreams too big, he pushed his luck.
He tried to dance with a wiggly worm,
But oh dear Chuck! He took a turn!

He flipped and flopped, rolled down a hill,
Bouncing off a toadstool, what a thrill!
A wise old owl laughed with glee,
'Nutty tales are the best, you see?'

So Chuck decided to gather friends,
And host a party that never ends.
Squirrels, bunnies, and birds galore,
Danced with joy, laughter galore!

In the frolic and fun, he learned so well,
That every nut has a tale to tell.
So if you find a nut on a spree,
Join the party, it's the place to be!

Growth Rings of Time

In the forest deep, a squirrel did scheme,
To hoard all the nuts, or so it would seem.
But he tripped on a root, what a comical fall,
With nuts flying high, it was chaos for all.

A wise old oak watched with branches a-shake,
As the critters around made a merry mistake.
"Oh dear!" he laughed, with his leaves all a-quiver,
"These nuts are for munching, not dancing in river!"

Through seasons they'd grow, each pup and each friend,
A community forged, on laughter they'd depend.
Nature's own jest, in the heart of the park,
Where squirrels play tag, till the sky grows dark.

So next time you wander, and hear woodland cheer,
Remember the antics; stay close and hold dear.
For growth rings of time tell a story, it's true,
That laughter among friends is the best gift for you.

A Nut's Quiet Adventure

A little nut dreamed of a journey so grand,
To leave the safe shell, and explore foreign land.
He rolled down a hill, with a squeak and a spin,
But found a young robin, who said, "Where've you been?"

"I'm scaling the heights, on a quest for some fame!"
The robin just chuckled, "Are you nuts? What a game!"
But onward he rolled, through the grass and the haze,
Till he bumped into deer, who just stared in a daze.

They giggled and gawked, couldn't believe such a sight,
A nut on a mission, with all of his might.
"I've seen all your fancies, your birds and your hawks,
But wait till you see my nutty sidewalks!"

The sun set with laughter, a spectacle bright,
As friends joined together, in the glow of twilight.
A nut's quiet adventure, though silly it sounds,
Turned into a party, where joy knows no bounds.

The Little One's Legacy

A tiny seed dropped from a branch up so high,
With dreams of the sky, oh my, oh my!
It rolled and it tumbled, through laughter and fun,
Claiming 'I'll grow into something, just one!'

A crowd of small critters gathered around,
As the seed shared its hopes, in the sun, on the ground.
"One day I'll be big, a tree tall and proud!"
The friends all just giggled, it was silly and loud.

Through thick and through thin, with each little bloom,
The seed found its friends, and the heart of the room.
Though small in the start, oh the stories they'd weave,
In the shade of its branches, the world would believe.

The little one's legacy, though humble it seems,
Was a laughter and joy brought to all of their dreams.
From small things come greatness, in forests and more,
So cherish each moment, let laughter restore!

Echoes of the Woodland

In the heart of the glade, where the tall trees do sway,
A chorus of critters joined in their play.
With acorns like drums, they beat out a tune,
Under the watchful eye of the merry raccoon.

One day while they danced, a chipmunk ran fast,
With a slip and a trip, oh, his joy didn't last!
He tumbled and rolled, legs flailing about,
As laughter erupted, the woodland did shout.

From hedgehogs to moles, all joined in the fun,
Celebrating moments, as bright as the sun.
"Let's dance till we drop!" cried a wise old tortoise,
And the party proceeded, without any notice.

So echoes of woodland now tell the great tale,
Of dancing with friends, and a chipmunk's travails.
For laughter's the magic, wherever you roam,
In the woods and the fields, it's a heartwarming home.

The Hidden Journey of a Nut

In a cap of brown, a story unfolds,
A nut on a quest, brave and bold.
Bouncing down hills, dodging a fox,
Dreaming of growing into a great oak box.

With squirrels in hats, and raccoons in suits,
He giggles at roots, and giggles at shoots.
Each twist and each turn, his laughter grows loud,
He's the nutty hero, a nutty proud crowd.

In puddles he splashes, without any care,
Waving at critters, all dancing in air.
His journey so wild, it's hard to believe,
That a nut full of joy can dream and achieve.

With a final big bounce, he lands on the ground,
And rolls past a flower, with a wink and a sound.
"I'm off to be mighty, just wait and you'll see!"
A nut on an adventure, forever so free.

Chronicles of the Green Realm

In the heart of the glade, the tales overlap,
Where mushrooms wear shoes and fairies take naps.
A leaf on the breeze whispers secrets galore,
While acorns hold court and legends explore.

The grasshoppers argue the best way to hop,
As the ladybugs giggle, they can't seem to stop.
"Who's the best flyer?" a beetle will shout,
While fireflies spark up and join in, no doubt.

Beneath a tall oak, a council convenes,
The ants in their suits are just cracking the scenes.
They trade off their stories, each funnier still,
"In the shade of my leaf, you must hear of my spill!"

With laughter like music, they spin every yarn,
From silly missteps to a clash on the lawn.
In the green realm they thrive, so free and so bright,
In the chronicles spun under soft moonlight.

Secrets of the Silent Grove

In the silent grove where the shadows hold sway,
A nut found a secret or two on the way.
He spotted a snail with a hat made of cheese,
Who wiggled and giggled as he bent with the breeze.

"What's this?" said the nut, with a wink and a grin,
"A party of critters? Oh, let's dive right in!"
Hedgehogs with ties played a piano of sticks,
And even a rabbit perfected his tricks.

As night softly fell, stars twinkled bright,
The nut and his friends danced a wild, silly flight.
They flopped and they rolled, twirling with glee,
The secrets of silence turned into a spree.

So next time you wander through groves lost in thought,
Remember the joy that a simple nut brought.
With laughter and friendship, they turned dark to light,
In a silent grove, fun bloomed overnight.

The Forest's Forgotten Narratives

Once upon a time, in a forest so wide,
Where the trees held stories that they could not hide.
A nutton so charming, with mischief to spare,
Danced past ancient whispers, charming and rare.

He tumbled right past a wise old tree,
"Hey, watch where you're rolling, or you'll trip over me!"

The mushrooms chuckled, the ferns swayed with glee,
Finding humor in tales of the nut's wild spree.

As moonlight glimmered on branches up high,
He shared tales of high-flying squirrels in the sky.
The beetles brought snacks, and the crickets sang tunes,
With laughter that echoed beneath glowing moons.

Forgotten narratives came to life with delight,
In a forest of laughter, from morning to night.
So if you hear chuckles, or snickers, or squeals,
It's nutty adventures, that's just how it feels.

Stories from the Woodland Floor

In a cozy nook, a nut did sway,
Telling tales of the fowl and the sway.
A squirrel pranced, with a twitchy tail,
'Bet you can't dance!' it dared without fail.

With a tiny grin, the nut took a chance,
And rolled down the hill in a clumsy prance.
The critters laughed, what a sight to see,
As the nut tumbled on, wild and free!

A chipmunk yelled, 'Now, who's the best?'
The nut replied, 'I'm not like the rest!
I've got stories to share, I can sway and spin,'
But they just chuckled; it wasn't a win.

So each little nut that resides on the floor,
Holds court for the critters with tales to explore.
With laughter in the air, they sit, and they chat,
Under the canopy, what fun where they're at!

The Nut that Dreamed of Greatness.

There was a nut, so plump and round,
Who dreamed of a kingdom where he'd wear a crown.
He wished to be great, to be daring and bold,
Not just a snack for the critters to hold.

He climbed on a leaf, raised high in the air,
'Look at me, folks, I'm beyond compare!'
But a bird swooped down, and the nut fell with a thud,
And the worm below said, 'Well, isn't that crud?'

He dusted himself, and thought with a snap,
'Being a snack, well, that's quite the trap!'
So he called all his friends, said, 'Listen, my crew,
Let's join together and create something new!'

They formed a parade, a nutty brigade,
Rolling and laughing in the sun and the shade.
And though he was small, he found quite a spark,
For greatness is laughter, not just leaving a mark!

Tiny Tales from the Oak

Under the oak, where stories unfold,
Tiny tales of silliness and gold.
A wee little nut made a wondrous wish,
To grow into something like a mighty fish!

He called for the rain, but it missed by a mile,
Instead, he got puddles that made him beguile.
A frog on a log said, 'Why wish for a sea?
You're a nut, my dear chap, you're as nutty as me!'

The oak shook with laughter, his branches did sway,
As the nut finally learned to just enjoy the play.
With friends all around and mischief to share,
He found all his dreams were right there in the air!

So remember, dear friends, when dreams start to soar,
There's magic in laughter on the woodland floor.
As the stories keep growing with each giggling chat,
Life's far more fun when you're silly like that!

Whispers Beneath the Canopy

Amidst the moss and leaves that twirl,
A nut squeaked out, 'What a world, what a whirl!'
With each stroll that passed, he'd wiggle and wink,
Spouting tales of a frog who danced on the brink.

Beneath the tall trees, they'd gather around,
To hear every word with laughter unbound.
The chipmunks would giggle, the birds would all cheer,
As the wise little nut drew them near without fear.

'What do you think, shall we make it a game?
Let's act out my stories and all take a name!'
And soon they were marching, a wild troupe of fun,
With a nut as their leader under the sun.

So remember, dear friends, next time you roam,
Let laughter and stories be part of your home.
For every little nut knows, just so you see,
Joy's woven in whispers beneath every tree!

The Language of Leaves

In the rustle of trees, whispers abound,
Secrets of nature, rich and profound.
Leaves gossip softly, like friends in a park,
Their tales grow wild, as day turns to dark.

One leaf tells another, 'Did you see that fall?
The squirrel in sneakers? Oh, he's got gall!'
They chuckle and cackle, with humor so spry,
As the wind steals their jokes and sends them up high.

The maple says, 'Wait! A rumor I heard,
Some grass claims it dances, oh how absurd!'
Laughter erupts, they wiggle and shake,
As birds join the fun, they all start to quake.

So next time you wander through woodlands so green,
Listen to leaves, you'll hear quite the scene.
For nature has humor, in sunlight and breeze,
With stories and giggles that sway through the trees.

Leafy Legends of Longevity

There once lived a leaf, who had wisdom galore,
He claimed he was ancient, from times long before.
The others would gather, their eyes opened wide,
As he spun his tall tales, with leafy pride.

He spoke of a squirrel, who once wore a cape,
Who fought off the crows, in a daring escape.
With acorns for armor, he took on a foe,
And conquered the skies, oh what a show!

But the best of his tales was about a great tree,
Who danced by the moonlight, a sight to see.
With roots in the ground, he twirled without care,
While the forest all giggled, a whimsical affair.

So remember, dear friends, when you're under the shade,
That leaves tell of legends, in their own leafy parade.
With humor and mischief, they brighten the day,
In stories of yore, that never decay.

The Nut that Flew

A nut once proclaimed, 'I long for the skies!
I've heard of the eagles, and how they can fly!'
The other nuts laughed, 'You're just round and small,
What makes you think you can answer the call?'

But undeterred, he plotted a scheme,
To race with the wind, oh what a wild dream!
He perched on a branch, with wings made of leaves,
And shouted, 'Just watch as I fly through the eaves!'

With a push and a bounce, he launched into air,
But mid-flight he faltered, with flops everywhere.
He tumbled and spun, landing soft with a thud,
Surrounded by friends, who roared with a flood.

'You gave it a go,' said the walnut so wise,
'You may not have soared, but you melted our sighs.'
And so with a chuckle, they gathered around,
To celebrate nutty dreams, joyfully found.

Stories Written in the Wind

In the whispering wind, tales drift and dart,
Of things that were once, and ideas that start.
A breeze shared a secret, of a frog at the pond,
Who fancied himself as a leaping beyond.

He'd train with the daisies, on flips and on spins,
While dragonflies cheered, as he practiced his wins.
Then one sunny morn, he leapt with such flair,
But landed in mud, oh the laughter in air!

The wind swirled around, with giggles and glee,
As birds swooped in close, 'Come join the jubilee!'
They danced over puddles, all splashing with joy,
With a chorus of chirps for that leaping young boy.

So remember, dear friends, next time clouds align,
That laughter is lifted, in nature's design.
For every breeze carries, a story or two,
When listened to softly, they'll tickle you too.

www.ingramcontent.com/pod-product-compliance
Lightning Source LLC
Chambersburg PA
CBHW071830160426
43209CB00003B/268